The Brooklyn Bridge
The Chesapeake Bay Bridge-Tunnel
The Coos Bay Bridge
The Evergreen Point Bridge
The Frankford Avenue Bridge

The Golden Gate Bridge
The Mackinac Bridge
The Royal Gorge Bridge
San Francisco–Oakland Bay Bridge
The Verrazano–Narrows Bridge

AMERICA'S TOP 10 BRIDGES

By
Edward Ricciuti

Published by Blackbirch Press, Inc.
260 Amity Road
Woodbridge, CT 06525

©1998 Blackbirch Press, Inc.
First Edition

Printed in the USA

10 9 8 7 6 5 4 3

Library of Congress Cataloging-in-Publication Data
Ricciuti, Edward R.
    America's top 10 bridges / by Edward R. Ricciuti.
        p. cm.—(America's top 10)
    Includes bibliographical references and index.
    Summary: Introduces ten famous American bridges: the Verrazano-Narrows, San
Francisco-Oakland Bay, Frankford Avenue, Royal Gorge, Golden Gate, Evergreen Point,
Chesapeake Bay, Mackinac, Coos Bay, and Brooklyn Bridge.
    ISBN 1-56711-197-1 (lib. bdg. : alk. paper)
    1. Bridges—United States—Juvenile literature. [1. Bridges] I. Title. II. Series.
TG148.R5 1998   96–52998
388—dc21   CIP
                                                                                      AC

BLACKBIRCH PRESS, INC.
WOODBRIDGE, CONNECTICUT

AMERICA'S TOP

10

BRIDGES

Manhattan

East River

Brooklyn Bridge

Brooklyn

The Brooklyn Bridge

★ ★ ★ ★ ★ ★ ★ ★ ★ ★ ★ ★ ★ ★ ★

No American bridge has been more celebrated in songs, stories, and poetry than the Brooklyn Bridge. This grand structure spans New York City's East River and connects the boroughs of Brooklyn and Manhattan. The bridge is known for the majesty of its stone approaches and granite towers. Between its towers, the Brooklyn Bridge has a main span of 1,595 feet, which made it the world's longest suspension bridge when it was completed in 1883. Suspension bridges have roadways that hang by steel "suspenders" from steel cables. These, in turn, are held up by a pair of towers.

When the bridge was built, Brooklyn and New York were separate cities. Both were thriving business centers. The only way to cross the East River that flowed between them was by ferry. During the very cold winter of 1866–67, ice made it difficult to run the ferry service, and the decision was made to build a bridge over the East River.

J.A. Roebling and his son designed the Brooklyn Bridge using technology that was brand new at the time. It was the first suspension bridge to hang from cables of steel wire. With an average clearance of 133 feet above high tide, the bridge was high enough to allow ocean-going vessels— both sailboats and steam-powered ones—to pass underneath.

Almost as soon as the bridge was opened, it became a popular spot for weekend strollers. In 1964, the bridge was designated a National Historic Landmark.

Location: Between Brooklyn and Manhattan in New York City
Type: Suspension
Body of water spanned: East River
Opened: May 24, 1883
Length: Suspended structure 3,400 feet; main span 1,595 feet
Construction time: 13 years
Cost: $9 million
Fun fact: The main cables of the bridge are 16 inches thick.

Opposite page:
The Brooklyn Bridge is known for the beauty of its granite towers.

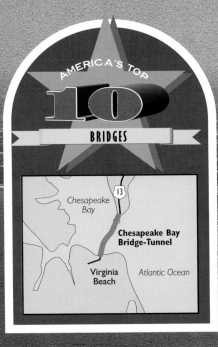

AMERICA'S TOP

10

BRIDGES

Chesapeake
Bay

13

**Chesapeake Bay
Bridge-Tunnel**

Virginia
Beach

Atlantic Ocean

The Chesapeake Bay Bridge-Tunnel

★ ★ ★ ★ ★ ★ ★ ★ ★ ★ ★ ★ ★ ★

The Chesapeake Bay Bridge-Tunnel (also known as the Lucius J. Kellam, Jr., Bridge-Tunnel) is considered one of the greatest engineering projects in the world. It is also the world's largest bridge-tunnel. It connects the Eastern Shore of Virginia with the rest of the state. The Eastern Shore is located at the southern end of a peninsula—land that juts out into the water. This part of Virginia is cut off from the rest of the state by Maryland and Delaware, to the north, and by the mouth of Chesapeake Bay, to the south. When the Chesapeake Bay Bridge-Tunnel opened in 1964, motorists could drive from the Eastern Shore to mainland Virginia in only 25 minutes.

This great engineering achievement is a combination of trestles, 2 tunnels, and 2 high-level bridges. Together they stretch 17.6 miles across the entrance to Chesapeake Bay. The waterways over the tunnels form an important route for naval vessels heading for bases on the Virginia mainland. Tunnels were built because in time of war, bridges in that area might be destroyed, blocking the channel.

The 2 high-level bridges are over smaller shipping channels. The North Channel Bridge, the largest, provides a clearance of 75 feet for passing ships. The other, the Fisherman Inlet Bridge, has a 40-foot clearance.

Construction of the bridge-tunnel began in the fall of 1960 and took over 4 years. In 1987, the bridge-tunnel was officially named for Lucius J. Kellam, Jr., who led the effort to build it.

Location: Between Hampton Roads, Virginia, and Virginia's Eastern Shore
Type: Complex of concrete trestles, 2 tunnels, and 2 high-level bridges
Bodies of water spanned: Chesapeake Bay and Atlantic Ocean
Opened: April 15, 1964
Length: Shore-to-shore: 17.6 miles
Construction time: 42 months
Cost: $200 million
Fun fact: Since it opened, more than 60 million vehicles have crossed the bridge-tunnel.

Opposite page:
The Chesapeake Bay Bridge-Tunnel is the largest bridge-tunnel in the world.

AMERICA'S TOP

10

BRIDGES

Pacific
Ocean

101

Coos Bay Bridge

North
Bend

Coos Bay

The Coos Bay Bridge

This spectacular bridge (also known as the McCullough Bridge) across Oregon's Coos Bay was designed as a major link in coastal Highway 101 along the Oregon coast. Construction of the bridge began in 1934, on July 25. It was the last of 5 bridges built for Highway 101 between 1934 and 1936. When it was opened, the Coos Bay Bridge was the longest in the state. Today, the bridge is still a vital link in the Oregon highway system. An average of 15,900 vehicles per day cross the single deck of this bridge.

The structure is named after its designer, Conde B. McCullough, a well-known highway engineer. He played a key role in creating the state's modern highway system. The bridge across Coos Bay opened in 1936. To make the bridge, workers used 51,000 cubic yards of concrete, 2,205 tons of reinforced steel, and 3,635 tons of structural steel. In 1947, a year after McCullough died, the bridge was dedicated to his memory. It is one of the few bridges in the world to be named after its designer.

The Coos Bay Bridge is known for its clean design, which is very pleasing to the eye. The bridge has 3 spans. The center—the major portion of the bridge—is a 1,709-foot cantilever structure. Its center span is 793 feet long between the piers. This part of the bridge has a clearance of 180 feet above the water, to allow large ships to pass beneath it. This main bridge is connected to shore by 13 spans supported by reinforced-concrete arches.

Location: North Bend, Oregon
Type: Cantilever; concrete arch
Body of water spanned: Coos Bay
Opened: August 9, 1936
Length: Cantilever with span 1,709 feet; total 5,305 feet
Construction time: 2 years
Cost: $2.9 million
Fun fact: Building the bridge required a total of 789,040 hours of work.

Opposite page:
The center span of the Coos Bay Bridge is a cantilever structure.

AMERICA'S TOP
10
BRIDGES

Seattle

Lake
Washington

Evergreen
Point Bridge

90

The Evergreen Point Bridge

The Evergreen Point Bridge—7,578 feet in length—is the longest floating bridge in the world. It was the second floating bridge built across Lake Washington and was opened in 1963. The lake lies between the coastal city of Seattle, Washington, and the inland part of the state. The first bridge built across the lake was also a floating bridge. After it opened in 1940, travel to Seattle became much easier for people living on the eastern shore of Lake Washington, and the towns there grew in population. Traffic became too heavy for the existing bridge to handle alone. A second floating bridge was planned, to be built south of the first one. It would extend from Seattle to Evergreen Point, near Bellevue. Construction of the Evergreen Point Bridge began in 1960. Almost exactly 3 years later, it was opened to traffic.

The bridge consists of a floating portion that is linked to land on either end by short, ordinary bridges. The floating portion of the bridge is constructed of rectangular concrete sections called pontoons. The pontoons float in a line, partly covered by water, like a boat or barge. Each of the 19 main pontoons is 360 feet long and weighs 4,725 tons. The pontoons are linked by cables to 58 concrete anchors on the lake bottom. Near the center of the floating portion is a drawbridge that opens in an unusual way. Two pontoons back away from each other and withdraw under 2 spans of the bridge, which are lifted more than 7 feet into the air. This creates an opening 200 feet wide through which ships can pass.

Location: Between Seattle, Washington, and the eastern shore of Lake Washington
Type: Pontoon
Body of water spanned: Lake Washington
Opened: August 28, 1963
Length: Floating structure 7,578 feet
Construction time: 3 years
Cost: $34 million
Fun fact: A total of 115,500 vehicles cross over the 4-lane bridge each day.

Opposite page:
The Evergreen Point Bridge was built as a floating bridge because the bottom of Lake Washington was too muddy for a standard bridge.

AMERICA'S TOP
10
BRIDGES

Philadelphia

Pennypack Creek

Upper
Holmsburg

Frankford Avenue

Frankford
Avenue
Bridge

Holmsburg

The Frankford Avenue Bridge

★ ★ ★ ★ ★ ★ ★ ★ ★ ★

Some bridges deserve recognition because of their immense size, the great waters they span, or the large numbers of vehicles that cross them. The Frankford Avenue Bridge is small. It crosses a little stream in northeastern Philadelphia. Only about 13,700 vehicles pass over it daily. Even so, in September 1996, a crew filming a documentary for Japanese television on the world's great bridges came to this little stone crossing over Pennypack Creek. They were there because of the age of the Frankford Avenue Bridge—it was built in 1697.

Planning for the bridge began in the 1690s, when a highway called the Great Frankford Road was built between Philadelphia and New York City. Local men provided plenty of help in building the bridge. Anyone who lent a hand did not have to pay taxes.

The Frankford Avenue Bridge is made of stone and is supported by arches. The design of the bridge is ancient, dating back to the Romans. It has 3 spans. Two are 24 feet long and the third is 13 feet long. In 1893, in order to widen and strengthen the bridge so that trolleys could cross it, another bridge was built and attached alongside it. The original bridge is still there, however, and looks almost as it did in 1690.

The Frankford Avenue Bridge was an important crossing during the time of the American Revolution. Troops of the Continental Army marched across it. And in 1789, on April 30, George Washington crossed the bridge as he traveled to New York City for his presidential inauguration.

Location: Philadelphia, Pennsylvania
Type: Stone arch
Body of water spanned: Pennypack Creek
Opened: 1697
Length: Main bridge 61 feet
Fun fact: According to legend, the bridge was placed where it is so that William Penn, founder of Pennsylvania, could reach his summer home outside Philadelphia with ease.

Opposite page:
Philadelphians recently celebrated the 300th anniversary of the Frankford Avenue Bridge.

AMERICA'S TOP

10

BRIDGES

Marin County

101

**Golden
Gate Bridge**

*Golden Gate
Strait*

San Francisco

The
Golden Gate Bridge

★ ★ ★ ★ ★ ★ ★ ★ ★ ★ ★ ★ ★ ★

The Golden Gate Bridge is recognized by the American Society of Civil Engineers as one of the 7 civil engineering wonders of the world. When it opened in 1937, the bridge had the longest main span of any suspension bridge in existence. It held that record until the completion of the Verrazano–Narrows Bridge in 1964. The Golden Gate Bridge links San Francisco, with California's Marin County. It spans Golden Gate, a strait—or narrow water passage—between San Francisco Bay and the Pacific Ocean.

Work on the Golden Gate Bridge began in 1933. Four years later, President Franklin D. Roosevelt announced to the world that the bridge was open by pressing a telegraph key at the White House.

The job of building the bridge, whose towers stand 746 feet above the water, was difficult and dangerous. The Golden Gate Strait is swept by fierce currents and tides. For much of the year, fog cloaks the bay every day. Many safety precautions had to be taken. Workers who had to climb to great heights were put on special diets to prevent dizziness. A huge safety net was slung beneath the bridge. It saved the lives of 19 workers who fell off the bridge. Then, in 1937, on February 17, disaster struck. A scaffold gave way, and broke through the net. Ten men died in the accident.

Work on the 5-lane Golden Gate Bridge continues. In the mid-1990s a project to strengthen it against earthquakes was begun.

Location: Between San Francisco and Marin Counties, California
Type: Suspension
Body of water spanned: Golden Gate Strait
Opened: May 28, 1937
Length: Suspended structure 6,450 feet; main span 4,200 feet
Construction time: 53 months
Cost: $35 million
Fun fact: The bridge has 80,000 miles of wire in its cables.

Opposite page:
The Golden Gate Bridge is a landmark of the San Francisco Bay area.

AMERICA'S TOP

10

BRIDGES

St. Ignace

Straits of Mackinac

Mackinac Bridge

75

Mackinaw City

The Mackinac Bridge

The Mackinac Bridge, in Michigan, soars over the Straits of Mackinac (pronounced MACK-in-naw). Its 2 main towers reach 552 feet above the surface of the cold, blue water. The maximum clearance for ships passing under the bridge—many of them huge freighters—is 155 feet. The bridge is noted for its length as well as its height. Its main span is the second-longest in the United States.

The Straits of Mackinac, which link Lake Michigan and Lake Huron, separate southern Michigan from the northern part of the state. The straits are up to 290 feet deep, and during the winter, the surface of the water is whipped by storms and covered with floating ice. It is no wonder that before it opened in 1957, the Mackinac Bridge was called "the bridge that couldn't be built."

Building the steel and concrete structure took more than 3 years. Construction began in the spring of 1954, when workers started on the foundations of the piers that would support the towers. Almost 1 million tons of concrete were poured to make the piers, which stood as much as 210 feet below the water.

The 3,500 workers at the bridge site had to take advantage of the good weather in spring, summer, and early fall. By late fall, storms blasted the Great Lakes region. During the height of the winter, construction was shut down completely. When the Mackinac Bridge was finally opened, the northern and southern parts of Michigan were united by a roadway for the first time.

Location: Between St. Ignace and Mackinaw City, Michigan
Type: Suspension
Body of water spanned: Straits of Mackinac
Opened: November 1, 1957
Length: Suspended structure 8,614 feet; main span 3,800 feet
Construction time: 41 months
Cost: $99.8 million
Fun fact: In order to build the bridge, workers used 4.9 million steel rivets, 1 million steel bolts, and, for the main cables, 42,000 miles of wire.

Opposite page:
The Mackinac Bridge soars above the icy Straits of Mackinac.

AMERICA'S TOP
10
BRIDGES

Parkdale ←

Arkansas River

Royal Gorge
Bridge

Royal Gorge

Cañon City →

The
Royal Gorge Bridge

★ ★ ★ ★ ★ ★ ★ ★ ★ ★ ★ ★ ★ ★

The Royal Gorge Bridge, in south-central Colorado, is considered the highest suspension bridge in the world. It spans a gorge—a narrow passage with steep, rocky sides—created by the swirling waters of the Arkansas River, 1,053 feet below. Unlike most other bridges, the one spanning Royal Gorge was intended to be a tourist attraction.

The Royal Gorge first attracted major attention in 1877, after silver was discovered at Leadville, to the north. Two railroad companies, the Santa Fe and the Denver & Rio Grande, fought over the right to lay track across the gorge. The courts awarded the rail route to the Denver & Rio Grande Railroad Company.

Traveling by train over the gorge soon became a popular activity. Even President Theodore Roosevelt was a frequent visitor. In 1907, the U.S. Congress turned the gorge over to Cañon City for a municipal park.

During the 1920s, a Texan named Lon Piper received permission to build a bridge over the gorge and operate it as a tourist attraction. Construction of the bridge began in June 1929 and was finished in only 6 months. The first step was to pour a concrete abutment on each rim of the canyon to support the ends of the bridge. Then 2 towers were erected. Next, two 300-ton cables were stretched between the towers and to each abutment.

The bridge is now part of an amusement complex. Since it was first opened, millions of people have crossed the bridge on foot, in automobiles, and on a trolley.

Location: 8 miles west of Cañon City, Colorado
Type: Suspension
Body of water spanned: Arkansas River
Opened: December 6, 1929
Length: Suspended structure 1,260 feet; main span 938 feet
Construction time: 6 months
Cost: $350,000
Fun fact: Even though most of the workers who built the bridge were local men with no experience, there were no major accidents.

Opposite page:
The Royal Gorge Bridge spans the Arkansas River, 1,053 feet below.

AMERICA'S TOP

10

BRIDGES

San Francisco–
Oakland Bay
Bridge

80

Oakland

San
Francisco

San Francisco Bay

The
San Francisco–Oakland Bay Bridge

★ ★ ★ ★ ★ ★ ★ ★ ★ ★ ★ ★ ★

The American Society of Civil Engineers has designated the San Francisco–Oakland Bay Bridge a National Historic Civil Engineering Landmark. The structure is actually 3 bridges— 2 suspension bridges and 1 cantilever bridge.

The construction of the bridge, which began in July 1933, was an immense and difficult job. This was partly because of the width of the bay, which is about 5 miles. Water depth was also a problem. Concrete for the piers supporting the bridge was poured to a depth of 218 feet, 33 feet deeper than concrete had ever been poured.

The 2 suspension bridges were built over the western part of San Francisco Bay that is 2 miles wide. They were connected by a huge "island" of concrete. The suspension bridges were extended to Yerba Buena Island, in the middle of the bay. There, engineers designed a tunnel that connected it to the cantilever bridge on the Oakland side. Construction of the bridge began in 1933 and was finished in the fall of 1936, six months ahead of schedule. While building the bridge, workers pulled up a large tooth of a prehistoric mammoth, which had been at the bottom of the bay! The bridge was officially opened by President Franklin D. Roosevelt, who pressed a button in Washington that turned on a green "go" signal light. At the signal, 3 columns of automobiles started over the bridge.

Part of the bridge collapsed during the earthquake of October 1989, and was repaired and reopened the next month. Now, about 275,000 vehicles per day travel over the bridge's 2 levels.

Location: Between Oakland and San Francisco, California
Type: Suspension; cantilever
Body of water spanned: San Francisco Bay
Opened: November 12, 1936
Length: Suspension 2,310 feet; cantilever 10,176 feet
Construction time: 40 months
Cost: $77 million
Fun fact: During peak traffic, 9,000 vehicles per hour cross the bridge.

Opposite page:
The San Francisco–Oakland Bay Bridge spans the 5-mile width of San Francisco Bay.

AMERICA'S TOP

10

BRIDGES

The Narrows

278

Brooklyn

Staten Island

**Verrazano–
Narrows Bridge**

Atlantic Ocean

The Verrazano–Narrows Bridge

★ ★ ★ ★ ★ ★ ★ ★ ★ ★ ★ ★ ★ ★

The Verrazano–Narrows Bridge, in New York City, has the longest main span of any suspension bridge in North America. It is huge, with 2 towers that are 693 feet above the average high water level. The piers that support the towers reach down to a depth of 170 feet below the average high tide. Each massive tower weighs 27,000 tons and is held together by 3 million steel rivets and 1 million steel bolts.

The bridge is named after the Italian navigator Giovanni da Verrazano, the first European to sail into New York harbor. He entered the harbor in 1524 through a channel between Lower and Upper New York Bays. Today, this channel is called the Narrows.

The bridge has 2 levels, crossed by more than 60 million vehicles per year, traveling between the boroughs of Brooklyn and Staten Island. Each of the 4 cables that supports the bridge is almost 39 inches in diameter. And each cable contains a total of 26,108 steel wires. Together, the anchorages required more than 375,000 cubic yards of concrete. The base of each anchorage is 230 feet wide and 345 feet long, about the total area of 2 football fields placed alongside each other!

Great ships from around the world pass through the Narrows on their way to New York harbor. The largest of these pass easily under the immense Verrazano–Narrows Bridge. During an average tide, there is 228 feet of room between the bridge and the water.

Location: Between Staten Island and Brooklyn, in New York City
Type: Suspension
Body of water spanned: The Narrows
Opened: Upper level November 21, 1964; lower level June 28, 1969
Length: Suspended structure 6,690 feet; main span 4,260 feet
Construction time: 63 months
Cost: $320.1 million
Fun fact: The roadway of the Verrazano is 12 feet lower in summer—when the metal in the bridge expands—than in winter—when the metal contracts.

Opposite page:
The Verrazano–Narrows Bridge has the longest span of any North American bridge.

America's Top 10 Bridges are not necessarily the longest. Although length was a basis for inclusion, we also considered a bridge's historical significance and the challenges that it presented to engineers when it was built. Below are 10 additional important bridges.

More American Bridges

Bridge, *Type*, Location, *Main Span*.

Bayonne, *steel arch*, New Jersey, *1,652 feet*.

Bronx-Whitestone, *suspension*, New York, *2,300 feet*.

Comodore Barry, *cantilever*, Pennsylvania, *1,622 feet*.

Columbia River, *continuous truss*, Washington–Oregon, *1,232 feet*.

Francis Scott Key, *continuous truss*, Maryland, *1,200 feet*.

George Washington, *suspension*, New York–New Jersey, *3,500 feet*.

Mississippi River, *cantilever*, Louisiana, *1,575 feet*.

New River Gorge, *steel arch*, West Virginia, *1,700 feet*.

Ravenswood, *cantilever*, West Virginia, *1,723 feet*.

Tacoma Narrows, *suspension*, Washington, *2,800 feet*.

Glossary

abutments Supports, usually made of concrete, at either end of a bridge.

approach A roadway or trestle leading to a bridge.

cable Very strong rope made of wire.

cantilever bridge A bridge that has 2 sections—each one anchored to the shore. The sections extend over the water but don't meet. They are joined by a third section—the center span.

channel The deep part of a river or harbor.

clearance The space between the surface of the water and the span of the bridge.

main span The stretch of bridge between the towers.

pier A support under a bridge usually made of steel or concrete.

pontoon A floating structure that supports a floating bridge.

span The spread of the bridge between the abutments.

structural steel Steel designed for building the framework of bridges and buildings.

suspension bridge A bridge with a roadway that hangs by steel "suspenders" from steel cables, which are in turn held up by 2 towers.

trestle A braced frame used to support a bridge.

Further Reading

Ardley, Neil. *Bridges*. Ada, OK: Garrett Educational Corporation, 1990.

Doherty, Craig, and Katherine Doherty. *The Golden Gate Bridge*. Woodbridge, CT: Blackbirch Press, 1995.

Pelta, Kathy. *Bridging the Golden Gate*. Minneapolis: Lerner Publications Co., 1987.

Kent, Zachary. *The Story of the Brooklyn Bridge*. Chicago: Childrens Press, 1988.

Robbins, Ken. *Bridges*. New York: Dial Books, 1991.

Spagenburg, Ray, and Diane Moser. *The Story of America's Bridges*. New York: Facts On File, 1991.

Where to Get On-Line Information

Brooklyn Bridge http://romdog.com/bridge/brooklyn.html
Golden Gate Bridge http://www.goldengate.org
San Francisco–Oakland Bay Bridge http://www.sfmuseum.org/hist2/bbridge.html
Verrazano–Narrows Bridge http://www.mta.nyc.ny.us/BandT/bt.html/bridges/html

Index

Photo Credits

Cover and page 2: ©Bruce Glassman/Blackbirch Press, Inc.; cover and page 4: Courtesy of the Chesapeake Bay Bridge and Tunnel District; cover and page 6: Courtesy of the Oregon Tourism Commission; cover and page 8: Courtesy of the Washington State Department of Transportation; cover and page 10: ©Jim McWilliams/Jim McWilliams Photography; cover and page 12: ©Robert Holmes/California Division of Tourism; cover and page 14: Courtesy of the Michigan Travel Bureau; cover and page 16: Courtesy of Royal Gorge Bridge; cover and page 18: ©Kerrick James/San Francisco Convention and Visitors Bureau; cover and page 20: MTA Bridges and Tunnels photo.